BUILD RELATIONSHIPS AND MAKE ABUNDANT SALES

THE ULTIMATE GUIDE ON HOW TO EARN CUSTOMER LOYALTY AND SELL MORE IN THE AUTO INDUSTRY

EDDIE TIONG H M

PUBLISHER: EDDIE TIONG

I wish to dedicate this book to my late wife who passed away peacefully on 24th December 2019 after two years battling with her cancer. We sadly miss her.

CONTENTS

CHAPTER 1

INTRODUCTION

A successful organization needs to generate sales as they bring in the income to support different departments within the organization. For this reason, Management often rewards Sales Reps incentives to motivate them into generating more sales revenue for the Company. If the percentage of sales declines, the entire company suffers as a unit; we expect the Sales Department to be the lifeblood of a Company.

The Sales career is a fascinating profession. This differs from my previous career in Information Technology (IT) Auditing for over 16 years (my roles as an IT Auditor and in my later years as an IT Audit Manager) in top global accounting and other commercial firms.

I started my career in Sales by accident. I later found this career is more suited to my personality and nature. I first gained formal sales training and experience in Real Estate for a brief period. Then I worked in Holiday Ownership (also known as Timeshare) for over seven years and ended up as a Car Sales Rep selling different world-class brands like Hyundai, Nissan, Mitsubishi, Mazda, Jeep, Alfa Romeo, Toyota, and Subaru. Altogether, I have over 17 years' sales experience and have an MBA and a Bachelor of Commerce degree. Every organization I worked in, taught me new things, but the sale process and its values and principles behind sales are similar.

Many people regard sales as the most effective way of earning unlimited income. Sales professionals can either earn more or earn less.

In the years I worked for top global accounting firms as an IT Audit Manager in Deloitte, Singapore, and Arthur Andersen, Sydney, I noticed that the Managers and Partners in these firms are on a continuous lookout for more consulting jobs besides fulfilling their statutory duties to clock more chargeable hours and revenues for the firm.

CHAPTER 2

TARGET READERS

I am writing this book for future Sales Reps who want to learn how to sell cars. It is a must-read guide and it can be regarded as an excellent training manual for them. Seasoned Sales Reps, Sales Managers, Business Managers, and Dealer Principals in the car industry can also refer to it to refresh their sales techniques and strategies and to practise good guidelines on sales and management. Sales Reps and Management in other industries such as real estate, holiday, and retail can also benefit from reading this guide.

The book highlights tips on world-class leadership and management in the competitive car industry to make a point of difference. As sales are vital in all organizations, sales reps can use this book in any organization although I customize this book to the automotive industry. Drawing from my experience in sales, I aim to impart this experience to sell more of their products, be it cars, holiday ownership, consulting, or real estate.

CHAPTER 3

A DAY CYCLE IN A CAR SALES REP'S LIFE

A Day in the life of a Car Sales Rep usually begins by rearranging the car yard in a dealership, working as a team, moving and lining up cars so they look straight and attractive to prospects and customers.

Definition of prospects and customers in this book

Prospects are potential or prospective customers or leads. It could be a cold lead, a warm lead or a hot lead.

Customers are those who had already purchased a car from the dealership before, and they may want to upgrade their current car or buy another new car from the same dealership.

After tidying the yard, the Sales Manager has a meeting with his team. During this meeting, the Manager often asks Sales Reps on the number of firm appointments they have for the day. Discussion revolves around sales targets, sales incentives or rewards, work issues, date of going out of cars sold, estimated date of arrival of ordered cars, administration matters, and any other matters relating to sales.

After the meeting, the team often conducts sales training in the form of role-playing between a prospect and a Sales Rep on a six-point presentation of a model car.

To avoid staleness in the dealer's room, Sales Reps and the Sales Manager often rearrange cars in this room by key models to give a fresh look for prospects and customers. It displays these cars in their top state in terms of cleanliness and attractive outlook.

Some other key activities during the day for a Sales Rep are:

- To follow up customers in the sales database and prospects from other sources to make firm appointments;
- Taking incoming calls, enquiries on sales and car-related matters.
- Keeping customers informed on the estimated date of delivery for cars ordered;
- Inform the customers on the date of delivery for cars in stock unless there is a separate Delivery Department to take care of this;
- Managing and responding daily prospects' and customers' correspondences including sales quotes, issues, and enquiries;
- Improve their skills and knowledge through research, in house discussions, online and external courses;
- Always be on the show, ready to serve prospects and customers coming into the dealership and to sell them a car;
- To be proactive looking around the dealership for

tasks to improve the dealership's image.

For deliveries scheduled for the day, liaise with parties such as Detailing and After Market sections to get the car ready, inspected and address any issues before the customer arrives.

CHAPTER 4

A SALES PROCESS

I n every car dealership, there is a formal sales process for Sales Reps to adhere to. One can tailor a good Sales Process to a specific dealership requirement.

When a prospect walks into a car dealership, a Sales Rep should just let the person look at a car for a minute before approaching the person.

One should just greet and get to know the prospect or customer by engaging in conversation on topics of interest to them. The conversation should flow and be natural. A sound guide is for the first couple of minutes, to steer away from the subject on the car and more to make a friend. After that, only then Sales Reps should ask their prospects on the car they are after. If they ask about a specific model, Sales Reps can then go deeper to find out their needs, wants, and desires. At all times, Sales Reps should read the body language of their prospects or customers and adapt to make them feel comfortable.

A good acronym SPACED which I learned from my past training is used to remember a person's dominant buying motives. It stands for Safety, Performance, Appearance, Comfort/Convenience, Economy, and Dependability. By asking the prospect or customer the right questions, Sales

Reps could size up what their dominant buying motives are and then be able to customize their selling approach. The Sales Rep would then conduct a presentation around and inside the car with these motives in mind.

FAB (Features, Advantages, and Benefits) is an acronym often used during training to help present the car model of interest and its key features important to the prospect. For each of these key features, a focused Sales Rep would try to link the feature to its advantage and how it would benefit the prospect or customer during his presentation. For example, a "rain-sensing windshield wiper" is a **feature**, the **advantage** is the sensor turns on the car's wipers whenever it senses rain and the **benefit** to the prospective buyer is that he can focus on driving the car and not having to worry about the rain.

This customized approach would keep the prospect's emotions high throughout the sales process before talking on the price of the car and negotiating a deal.

A prospect may request for a valuation of his car; the following sub-process is a guide to follow before the prospect goes on a test drive. The Sales Rep should capture all the details of the car including photos of key areas inside and outside the car using the approved valuation application installed on their mobile phones and submit the valuation online. In this way, by the time the prospect or customer comes back from the test drive, the valuation result is ready.

In the old days, the Used Car Sales Manager performs the valuation based on a manual form capturing the car's details, sighting, and testing the car. This valuation approach is now outdated with the advancement of technology.

In most cases, the prospect's old car trade-in value is used to set off against the purchase price of their new car. There are cases that the prospect or customer just wants to sell his old car; the management could then issue a cheque to him on the agreed amount.

Managers or allowed staff or contractors would value the cars either based on the details filled in on the manual form or it based on an electronic application submitted as mentioned above.

After submitting the trade-in car valuation application online, the Sales Rep should offer the prospect or customer a test drive to show the features important to the prospect. If the prospect cannot come to the dealership for a test drive, the Sales Rep should go the extra mile and bring the car to the prospect's home for a test drive.

From my sales experience, on rare occasions, I can sense that a prospect is wasting my time. In such a situation, it is wise to consult the Sales Manager for the best course of action and to deny the person a test drive.

For a test drive, it is a good practice to use a consistent test drive route where possible. A test drive route should be at least 20 minutes and it should include where practically a highway and a road going uphill and downhill so that the prospect can test the car's key features and the Sales Rep can explain how these features work.

During the test drive, the Sales Rep should also do a trial close which allows the prospect to voice any concerns he has and if there are no material concerns, the Sales Rep can ask the person if it fits their budget, would he buy the car TODAY?

After the test drive, the Sales Rep should get the prospect seated, offer him a drink, and discuss whether the prospect is satisfied with the test drive. If the person likes the car, the Sales Rep would often fill in a sales order on the prospect's desired car model. The Sales Rep would then introduce him to the Customer Service Consultant (also known as the Aftermarket Representative). This is to work out a satisfactory package deal for the buyer. It is also good to change a prospect's chemistry by talking to another person in keeping his emotions high.

If the prospect has questions or objections, Sales Reps should try to overcome these objections early in the sales process. This is to make the prospect feel assured and at ease. Should Sales Reps need help to overcome a specific objection, they can seek their Manager's help. If the objection is over insufficient money, the Sales Rep can seek the help of a Business Manager to finance the purchase.

Once the Customer Service Consultant prices up an order package including the aftermarket products, the Sales Rep can then go back to the buyer and ask for the deal and conduct the final negotiation on the price.

If it satisfies the prospect with the refined package negotiated, the Sales Rep then draws up a contract with an estimated delivery date of the car. In the event, the car is on order (if no stock available), it is very important to give an estimated date of delivery and keep the customer posted during the waiting period. In some dealerships, there is a dedicated team just to manage the delivery process, in which case the delivery consultant would be in touch with the customer. This person would manage the entire delivery process until the customer leaves the dealership. In most organizations, the Sales Rep has to manage the delivery process besides selling cars.

If for whatever reason, a prospect cannot decide or decides not to buy the car on the day, the Sales Rep should get the Manager to double close the prospect before the person leaves the dealership. This is to maximize sales and networking opportunities.

CHAPTER 5

WINNING BEHAVIOR OF SALES REPS

S ales Reps should set clear and specific goals to know where they are heading and the desired outcomes that they want to achieve. It is important to know why one wants to achieve these goals and to visualize achieving them to make it motivating and desirable. There are lots of material out there on unique types of goals, on why and how to set goals.

Sales Reps should review their sales goals daily and put these goals at a visible spot to remind and motivate them.

Desired attributes of Sales Reps

Sales Reps should be professional at all times:

- They should promote a **pleasant and positive image** of themselves and that of the dealership;
- Sales Reps should maintain a neat, clean, friendly and smart image at all times during business hours;
- They should maintain **good hygiene**, for example, to keep their mouth fresh (avoid bad

breath) to create a good first impression to prospects and customers;

- Sales Reps should have a positive, serving, caring and maintain a "can-do" but humble **attitude**;

- They should be **well-trained** through in-house and external courses to serve the prospects and customers with excellence. I highlight the importance of training in a separate section (**);

- Sales Reps should always be **hungry for sales** to be of significant assets to their dealership;

- They should be **empathetic listeners**; listening to their prospects' needs, wants, desires and concerns;

- Sales Reps should learn to read their prospects' or customers' body language and ready to resolve their objections and uneasiness;

- They should be **hardworking, punctual, resourceful** and always be prepared at all times to handle different situations, and leave behind any personal problems at the dealership's front door once they start work for the day;

- Sales Reps should be **team players** sharing the load of their colleagues and that of the management; they should always lend a helping hand and go an extra mile whenever they are free;

- They should always maintain a calm and unhurried **demeanor/ composure** to avoid making silly mistakes through rushing and to avoid creating a tense environment in the presence of prospects and customers;

- Sales Reps should improve areas around the Dealership that require improvement during **downtime**, for example, to wipe off dusty cars in the showroom and lining up the cars in the yard to give it a smart look;
- They should mind their own business and steer away from **gossips and rumors and negativity**;
- Sales Reps should treat their prospects and customers at an arm length in dealings **separating personal from business**;
- They should be **experts in their field and know their products** and that of their competitors; at least for the key models of the cars they are selling;
- Sales Reps should be well versed with the **price of key models** and their **stock availability** at all times;
- They should always be sincere and act with **integrity and honesty** in their dealings with colleagues, prospects, and customers;
- Sales Reps should be in **constant contact with their customers** even after doing the deal. This is important where the cars are on order; one should keep the customers posted on the estimated date their cars would arrive and to inform them of any delays. This is to allay their concerns or fears of the unknown. Where delays result in conflicts, Sales Reps

should seek their Manager's help to resolve the conflict.

(**) Sales training

Sales training is a very broad category that includes the sales process, product knowledge, dealing with objections, open and closing skills, prospecting, territory management, listening skills, networking, presentation skills, and funnel administration, to highlight a few important topics. Sales Reps who ignore any of these items do so at their peril.

Sales training provides knowledge around specific topic areas their Sales Reps need to be proficient at their jobs. There is no point going out to sell, not knowing your product, the process to book the sale, how to deal with prospect concerns, or where you should go to find a prospect. Most companies invest heavily in sales training, especially with new Sales Reps. They cannot afford to dispatch the company's ambassadors poorly equipped. It is in their best interest to train them well.

The quality of sales training has an important impact on the success of Sales Reps.

No one could show expertise without the proper training that they gained in their career.

Hence, many salespeople are more than willing to submit themselves to sales training. They know that it would be one of the best ways to earn and achieve success.

So for those who cannot understand why sales training is important in a salesperson's career, here are some advantages of engaging in such sales booster activity.

1. It is of great help

Based on its basic concept, they created sales training to help the sales reps to horn their skills and improve their craft. It improves their ability to create more sales through the acquisition of advanced marketing strategies.

2. Molds better attitude

Another valuable thing about sales training is that it does not just focus on improving the skills and abilities of the salesperson as far as selling is concerned. Through this training, it also improves the attitude and behavior of the salesperson towards sales.

Sales training teaches them how to deal with customers, how to handle objections, and how to persuade people. Ordinary training programs rarely teach these things.

CHAPTER 6

WINNING BEHAVIOR OF MANAGEMENT

Managers, Dealers, and Partners (Management) belong to the "captain group." They are the leaders responsible for the success or failure of a car dealership. The members in it should strive to be brilliant leaders with a serving, caring, and protective attitude towards their staff. The following are some expected attributes and actions of good leadership or management in a dealership:

- Facilitate daily **meetings** to monitor sales targets, bonuses, deliveries, outstanding issues, and to provide sales incentives and rewards to motivate their Sales Reps, and to create a fun, loving, and rewarding environment;

- Always **encourage** their staff to give their best and to inspire and motivate them with phrases like "you can do it";

- They should **roll up their sleeves** and help where possible with the team in mind;

- **Defend their staff** and **help them** resolve disputes and/or conflicts whenever needed instead of abandoning them when they need your support;
- Ensure **cars in the car yard (s)** in the dealership are clean, polish, well-represented by key models, prices presented, and have at least half full tank fuel (for key models) ready for a test drive;
- Co-ordinates for older demo models and representative used cars for **professional photos** to be taken. The purpose is to advertise them on key sales websites (with high traffic track records) to attract enquiries from the public and generate sales from them;
- Show the dealership is **ready for business** to the public first thing in the morning with flags flying high;
- Ensure there is a **proper infrastructure**, including an efficient and effective fast IT network to support sales at least during business hours. There is nothing more frustrating for Sales Reps to find their computers are down or very slow when drafting up a quote or a sales contract;
- Enforce a policy of **double close by management or allowed staff** to minimize the loss of potential deals with prospects walking out the door;
- Develop and review **sales strategies, policies, and procedures** to enhance sales;

- Do not **burden Sales Reps** with unnecessary rules, procedures, policies, and changes that do not help to increase sales and to review on a periodic interval the effectiveness of rules, procedures, policies in increasing sales and to get rid of ineffective ones;
- Ensure an **up-to-date price list** for key models of cars for sale is always available;
- Prepare an **up-to-date list of demo cars and used cars** for sale.
- Co-ordinates internal and external **training** of staff.
- Practise catch staff **doing the right things** and praise or encourage them instead of catching you doing the wrong things or shame them in public;
- Guide, inspire, and **motivate** their staff rather than micromanage them;
- If there is a need to **correct and discipline staff**, do it on a one-to-one basis instead of in front of their colleagues;
- Ensure that the **product brochure** for each car model is current and available for prospects and customers;
- Ensure an **up-to-date inventory and price lists** of cars are available;
- Facilitate and organize **sales events** to boost sales revenue.
- Conduct **staff appraisals** on a periodic interval at least once a year.
- Monitor **customer satisfaction index** and re-

solve any issues to improve this index and the public image of the dealership;

· **Walk the talk, be a good example.**

I believe that Management in demonstrating the above attributes and actions would generate more loyalty, respect, and admiration among their staff, thus motivating them to give of their best. This would translate to higher revenues and lower staff turnover.

CHAPTER 7

COMMUNICATION

S ales Reps should horn their skills in communication. This is a critical skill contributing to their success in an organization. This skill serves as a lubricant to building great relationships.

Sales Reps should communicate with their managers and colleagues on all matters. This includes training, administration, and handling of issues including problems and conflicts, and communication with other departments such as the Service Department, Parts Department, and Detailing Department to get things done successfully and to the Company's satisfaction.

Sales Reps should daily call prospects and customers in the sales database to invite them into the dealership, with the focus on generating more sales. It requires clear and effective communication throughout the entire sales process described in Chapter 4. Top Sales Reps are excellent in making friends and generating an atmosphere of making the prospects and customers to like them.

Successful Sales Reps would maintain a habit of networking and providing quotes and wanting to help their prospects and customers.

After the signing of the sales contract, Sales Reps should

maintain constant contact with their customers to keep them informed on the progress of delivery of their cars and to advise them of any delays and issues. During the delivery process of their cars, Sales Reps should communicate any issues raised by their customers in their cars to their managers and resolve these issues immediately and to their customer's satisfaction. This is further elaborated in Chapter 8 on the delivery process.

Outstanding communication skills are also vital to management to get things done and to resolve issues. Management should be able to communicate with their staff in matters of training, discipline, policies, procedures, targets, and issues. It should also communicate between departments to get work done and to communicate any issues and resolutions thereof.

Managers are the faces of the organization they represent; therefore managers need to promote and cultivate a healthy image for the dealership through effective communication. There are many matters that management has to deal with include handling issues like the late arrival of cars, delivery issues, disputes in pricing and on the car purchased, resolving conflicts, coordinating sales events, on finance matters, negotiation of prices of cars, and so on.

A critical component of effective communication is listening skills. Both Sales Reps and Management should master this skill as this is important for their success.

CHAPTER 8

DELIVERY

All Sales Reps should liaise with the delivery (if it is a separate department), business and detailing departments, and check the cars at least an hour before the delivery time to identify any issues. Where there are issues, Sales Reps should resolve them before their customers arrive.

In some dealership, it is the practice or procedure that the car is covered for delivery with a piece of clean soft cloth presenting the new car with a nice welcoming look.

Another practice that some dealerships adopt is placing a bouquet of artificial flowers or a good looking big necktie band on the bonnet of the car for delivery. This is great for a photo opportunity as customers love photos taken on their new cars for memory or share their excitement with their friends and relatives.

Sales Reps should spend quality time with their customers going through the car's key features, helping them to take photos and videos of their new cars.

During the settlement process, Sales Reps should get the cheque payment from the customer and give it to their Business Manager to get a receipt for the payment made. Where the car is paid on a loan basis, Sales Reps should

EDDIE TIONG H M

introduce their customers to the Business Manager early to settle the finance on the car. Sales Reps should hand the receipt of payment to their customers and go over the car manuals and other related documents. They should then ask their customers for survey feedback on their experience with the dealership and with the Sales Rep. Where possible, Sales Reps should ask their customers for written feedback on Google if they have a Gmail account. This is important to gain publicity for the dealership and to attract others to the dealership.

In some dealerships, there is a practice to give a welcome purchase gift such as a hamper as part of its marketing. Sales Reps should give away this gift to maximize the opportunity to leave a warm and fuzzy feeling in their consumer's experience with the dealership. Happy and satisfied customers would surely be willing to introduce people in their circle of influence to purchase cars from your dealership.

CHAPTER 9

SPECIAL SALES EVENTS

Every dealership I worked for conducted special sales events, usually during the mid-year or year-end. The goal is to boost the dealership's sales revenue and to clear older stock. They advertise these events with a big electronic billboard and large banners advertisement outside the dealership glass wall to promote the upcoming sales to the walking and drive by traffic. The sales offers massive price cuts and other bonuses for sales sign-up during these events. Also, some dealerships would fence up the dealership yard and hang big promotional sales banners and advertisements on the fence. Some dealerships even announce the sales events over the radio to promote them.

During these events, many representative car models are clean up and display on the yards for sale; a lot more cars are on display during this period than on a normal day.

It is a common practice that a dealership would engage an external Consultant with an outstanding track record to facilitate these events. This external Consultant would provide:

- Training to Sales Reps to make these events a success.

- Motivate Sales Reps to give their best and teach them the winning approach;

- Provide scripts to guide Sales Rep on a winning phone call approach to invite guests to the dealership;

- Sales Reps would fill in on an appointment list (date, time, the model of car desired) and stick it on the wall as they make appointments for each day of sale. Management expects each Sales Rep to meet a target number of appointments per day;

- Desired sales targets to achieve by each Sales Rep for the sale event.

- Other related matters to increase sales.

Two days leading up to the sales event, Sales Reps would call the leads' names on the allocated list provided to them by the External Consultant or their Sales Manager. This list comprises customers from the current sales database extracted based on a set of criteria. The purpose of the call is to invite them to come in for the sales events to get them to buy more new cars or upgrade their existing cars.

During these sales events, management would hand out incentives and bonuses to reward Sales Reps that met set sales targets and to motivate and reward the top Sales Rep. Often management would put on a BBQ for staff and guests. The inviting aroma from the BBQ, the colorful balloons and announcements over the loud speaker all contributed to the creation of a festive atmosphere to promote sales during this period.

CHAPTER 10

REWARDS, INCENTIVES AND FUN

Most people love a bit of fun and like to celebrate milestones, such as birthdays, anniversaries, and achievements in their life with their loved ones and friends.

Sales Managers often give out incentives and rewards like gift cards, dinner, and movie vouchers to their team members for achieving certain sales targets. Most dealerships would offer free lunches to Sales Reps working on weekends. During the Christmas season, it is common for the dealership to hold an End of Year Dinner and even a dance function to celebrate and to thank the staff for their contribution to the dealership for the past year. In one dealership I worked at, the Dealer Principal would turn up in his huge American Ute with many legs of ham, giving each staff member a leg of ham to celebrate the breakup for the Christmas season.

Through all these small pleasant gestures, management

would instill respect, a good relationship, and loyalty of staff members to give their very best to the company or dealership.

CHAPTER 11

IMPACT OF COVID-19 ON CAR DEALERSHIPS

The Covid-19 (C-19) pandemic has had an enormous impact on all businesses in Australia and around the world. Their staff, prospects, and customers have to comply with the Government rulings of social distancing of 1.5 meters, keep good health hygiene in washing their hands frequently with soap, the mandatory wearing of masks, stay at home if tested with C-19, and to comply with the mandatory quarantine period if tested positive for C-19.

They designed all these measures to reduce the risks of the C-19 virus spreading and helps to flatten the curve and to suppress or to eliminate this virus.

For cars or parts ordered from countries badly hit by this virus, the implications of C-19 on a car dealership are huge/serious.

Under the current Stage 4 lockdown restrictions, the Showroom doors of car dealerships in Melbourne are closed, affecting sales.

The Government Job Keeper allowance policy to keep existing staff has helped to prop up struggling businesses including car dealerships from loss of revenue because of C-19.

CHAPTER 12

OTHER TIPS TO INCREASE SALES

Use Psychology to Increase Sales

Have you had trouble finding leads? The goal is to find prospects and customers interested in your cars, prompting them to purchase a car from your company. This is a task that is no easy feat unless you understand psychology. You can persuade them through various psychological techniques.

What types of psychology techniques should you use? The following are honest psychological techniques and not the work of a slick salesman. Anyone can try their hand at these techniques and maximize their leads and profits.

The three techniques include giving a gift, determining what your prospects and customers want, and presenting bounce back offers. Let's look at each technique in more detail:

Psychological Tip #1: Give a prospect or a customer a gift.

Giving a gift before you encourage a prospect to buy your product is highly effective. This method prompts your potential customer to buy more of your product at their initiation. Prospects and customers respond beneficially when they feel you are giving them a gift. Make sure you are truly giving a gift such as a mug, pen or a cap bearing the company's logo. A gift could be even in the form of offering free advice.

Giving gifts can also help you build your email list. You can give away gifts for contact information. Giving a gift is pre-selling and post-selling as well (also refers to Chapter 8 above on gifts given out during delivery). When prospects and customers trust you or your dealership, they are likely to buy more of your products. Being available and attentive to both your prospects and regular customers will increase your sales.

Psychological Tip #2: Determine what your prospects and regular customers want and present it to them. This is where dealerships spend lots of money advertising and marketing their cars through various media outlets: on online markets with a great track record, on TV, on banners hanging off the dealership glass window traffic facing, electronic billboard, brochures, and any other creative ideas that would generate leads for conversion to sales.

Psychological Tip #3: Bounce back offers are items or services that you will provide for free, or at a discount, once a customer has purchased your product. For example, you can entice customers by giving them a 10% coupon on their next purchase. The purpose of bounce back offers is not only to prompt your customer to buy in the first place but also to continue buying your products and services well into the future.

These three techniques are just a sample of the many ways you can reach a prospect and customer and convert a lead to a sale. Successful promoters incorporate these techniques into their marketing and promotion methods/skills.

4 Selling Techniques You Must Implement

It's difficult to reach your business goals if you do not have the right materials and/or the information to help your business reach the success it's capable of. These four insights will help you generate the business you've always dreamed of.

Exploring New Advertising Methods

The first sign that you might need to explore new marketing strategies is a sharp decline in the effectiveness of your advertisement campaign. You may have spent hard-earned cash on the advertisement and find them ineffective. Do not wait until your profits are plunging to hunt for new marketing strategies.

Wouldn't it be great if you could foolproof your selling techniques so that no more prospects and customers walking out with empty hands; no more profit disappearing into the thin air.

Here are 4 ways that will help you put money into your pocket and lengthen your current customer list.

1. Make It Easy

There's an adage that says variety is the spice of life, but too many choices can lead to indecision and procrastination by the customers. We all know what happens when prospects and customers procrastinate, you lose a sale.

When a prospect or customer walks into your business ready to purchase, and then they are confronted with several options they did not know were there. This will stop them from deciding straight out. If he is uncertain, you may lose a sale that was initially already in your pocket.

Make it easy for your prospects or customers to decide... yes, I'll buy it or no, I won't buy it. Yes and no decisions are a lot easier to make, and are more likely to put cash in the drawer.

2. Offer Several Ways to buy a product

Too many choices can overwhelm customers and cost you sales, but options of how to buy open up avenues for customers to purchase the product they've decided they need. They say there are different strokes for different folks... your prospects and customers don't all use the same methods to purchase something. It just makes sense that if the method they prefer is available, they'll be more likely to take advantage of it.

Convenience is the key to attracting buyers in today's fast-paced society. What will be the fastest and easiest for them... credit card, phone, fax, Internet, or cold hard cash?

3. Keep it Simple

You remember the frustration of spending 10 minutes pushing buttons on the phone just to get through an automated ordering service. When all you wanted to buy is one item! Maybe it is the time you have to click your finger raw, just to jump through the hoops of an online shopping cart, the temptation to just forget it is right there!

Do not frustrate your prospects and/or customers with intricate ordering procedures. Most likely, they just want to place the order in a few minutes and be done with it. Let them get frustrated, and they'll go elsewhere, or just abandon purchasing the car they came for.

4. Follow Up

One of my favorite catalog companies always closes out the sale with a special buy that is available only at the time of purchase. I'm not an impulsive shopper by any stretch of the imagination, but it stops me in my tracks every time. I know it's a onetime shot, and I consider whether I want or need it before I hang up the phone.

How many items would your prospects and customers buy if you were to follow up every sale with a special offer? Internet marketers have a world of options at their fingertips.

Boosting your sales numbers and profit dollars isn't as tough as it sounds. Implement these 4 simple selling techniques and watch your sales steadily climb... and just think... these do not cost you a penny!

CHAPTER 13

CONCLUSION

I n a dealership environment, when the Sales Reps and Management follow the above principles, tips, and guidelines of exemplary behavior and practices, the increase of revenues to the company would take care of itself.

BONUS CHAPTER

BIBLE VERSES ON KEY PRINCIPLES TO INCREASE SALES

T his chapter is a bonus chapter for those who do not find it offensive to refer to the Bible for guidance, search for wisdom, and sound principles. If it is offensive to you, please stop reading now. It gives you the gift of CHOICE in life.

Let us refer to the Bible (I call it the Old Book) for what it teaches about key principles that may help to increase sales. This is just an introduction; there are many other excellent principles in the Bible influencing behavior that would enhance sales.

Honest dealings

Proverbs 16:11 New International Version (NIV)

11 Honest scales and balances are from the Lord;
all the weights in the bag are of his making.

All Sales Reps should stick to honest dealings with their

prospects and customers. This is to avoid a bite back later from dishonest dealings which would lead to poor relationships; an approach which is short-sighted.

In summary, do the right thing by your fellow human beings and look for long-term relationships, referrals, and a customer who would return to you if they want to buy another product. This would lead to a generation of more sales for both Sales Reps and their dealership.

Relationships

Mark 12:30-31 NIV

30 *Love the Lord your God with all your heart and with all your soul and with all your mind and with all your strength.* 31 *The second is this: 'Love your neighbor as yourself.' There is no commandment greater than these.*

The principle here is to love your prospects and customers and the rest would take care of itself. I remember a former colleague who gave me sound advice to treat all walk-ins to a dealership like gold.

Interests of others

Philippians 2:4 NIV

4 *Each of you should look not only to your own interests, but also to the interests of others.*

This principle is about teamwork. Sales Reps and management should help each other achieve the overall good of the dealership while looking after their interests. This also would promote harmonious relationships within the company.

Acknowledgement

My special thanks to Ms. Anne Khoo and Mr. Khor (both are not professional Editors) for volunteering many hours of their time proofreading and making valuable observations & comments on my manuscript.

I also thank Mr. Gerry Robert and his team at Black Card Books for their mentoring and coaching, and for designing my beautiful book cover as part of the DIY Publishing Toolkit.

Most of all, I thank my heavenly Father for giving me the strength, tenacity, and wisdom to complete this book during the Covid-19 lockdown.

The author has an MBA and Bachelor of Commerce degrees and over 17 year's sales experience altogether. He has over nine years' experience in the Car Sales Industry in various major global car brands. He also has experience selling Holiday Ownership or known as Timeshare (over seven years) and worked as a Real Estate Representative for a short period. Before embarking on his sales career by accident, he had also worked as an IT Auditor and IT Audit Manager for over 16 years in top global accounting and other commercial firms.

ISBN 9798685832344

9 798685 832344